Learning About Landforms

Mountains

Chris Oxlade

Raintree is an imprint of Capstone Global Library Limited, a
company incorporated in England and Wales having its registered
office at 7 Pilgrim Street, London, EC4V 6LB – Registered company
number: 6695582

www.raintreepublishers.co.uk
myorders@raintreepublishers.co.uk

Edited by Rebecca Rissman, Daniel Nunn and Catherine Veitch
Designed by Steve Mead
Picture research by Elizabeth Alexander
Production by Victoria Fitzgerald
Originated by Capstone Global Library
Printed and bound in China

ISBN 978 1 4062 7226 0
17 16 15 14 13
10 9 8 7 6 5 4 3 2 1

British Library Cataloguing in Publication Data
A full catalogue record for this book is available from the
British Library.

Acknowledgements
We would like to thank the following for permission to reproduce
photographs: Alamy p. 7 (© paul kennedy); Getty Images pp.
24 (Slow Images/Photographer's Choice), 27 (Frans Lemmens/
The Image Bank), 29 (Val Corbett/Britain On View); Shutterstock
pp. 4 (© Pal Teravagimov), 13 (© Doug Matthews), 14 (© Sakarin
Sawasdinaka), 15 (© mrfotos), 16 (© Matteo Volpone), 17
(© Hank Shiffman), 18 (© Ramunas Bruzas), 19 (© Duncan Payne),
20 (© Jeffrey T. Kreulen), 21 (© Ssnowball), 22 (© my nordic), 23 (©
raeme Shannon), 25 (© Josh Schutz), 26 (© Jun Baby), 28 (© stefano
spezi).

Cover photograph of clouds moving away from the snowy sides of
Sernio mountain during winter in Paularo, Carnia reproduced with
permission of Corbis (© Gabriele Bano/SOPA RF/SOPA).

Every effort has been made to contact copyright holders of material
reproduced in this book. Any omissions will be rectified in subsequent
printings if notice is given to the publisher.

Contents

Some words are shown in bold, **like this.** You can find out what they mean by looking in the glossary.

What are landforms?

Earth is made up of different landforms. There are hills, mountains, **volcanoes**, valleys, islands and caves. A mountain is a landform that rises high above the land around it.

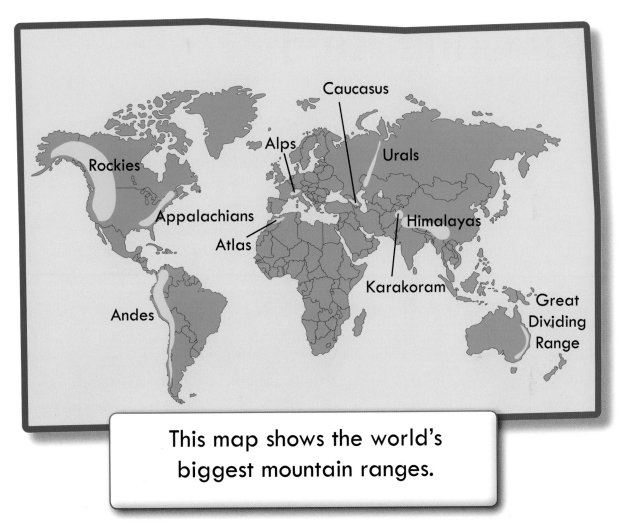

Caucasus

Alps

Urals

Rockies

Appalachians

Atlas

Andes

Himalayas

Karakoram

Great Dividing Range

This map shows the world's biggest mountain ranges.

Some mountains stand on their own, but most are in groups called **mountain ranges**. Mountain ranges such as the Himalayas stretch for many thousands of kilometres.

Rock and ice

Mountains come in many different shapes. Their parts have special names.

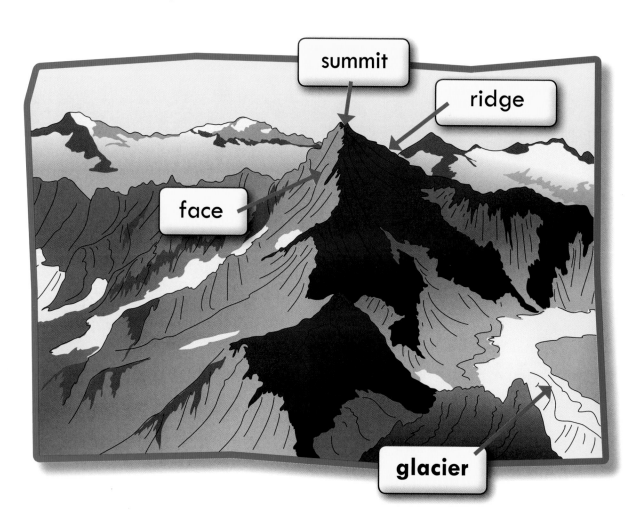

summit

ridge

face

glacier

snow line

The tops of most mountains are normally covered with snow and ice during winter, and sometimes all year round. The line around a mountain above which there is snow is called the snow line.

Earth's structure

The surface of Earth is called the **crust**. The crust is made up of huge, rocky slabs called **tectonic plates**. These parts of Earth are always moving.

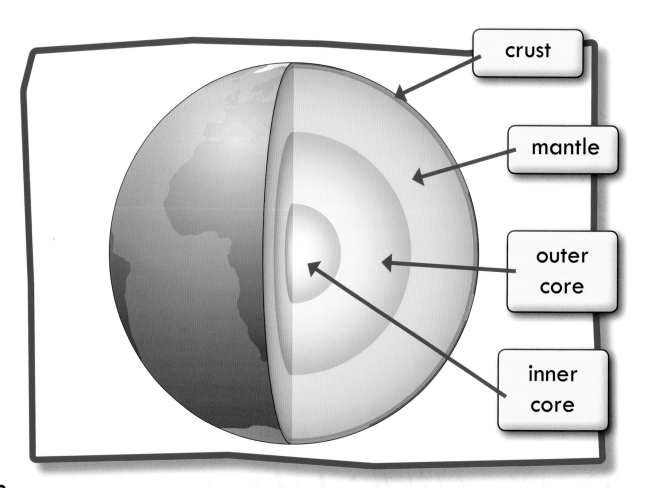

crust

mantle

outer core

inner core

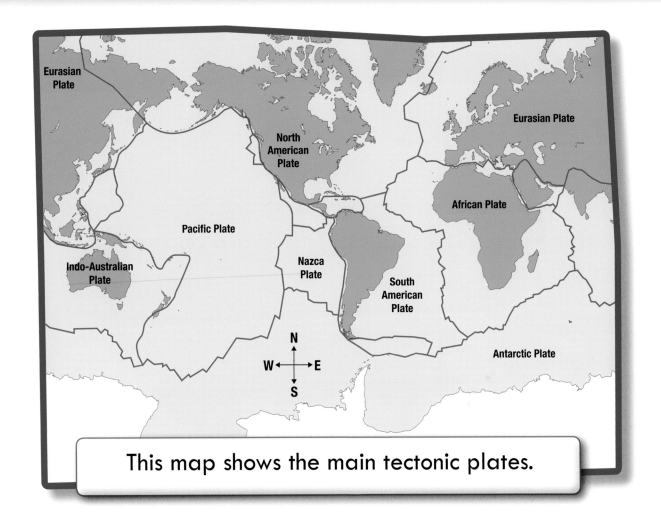

This map shows the main tectonic plates.

Most mountains are made when the tectonic plates push against each other. Rock is pushed up to make mountains.

Block and dome mountains

Block mountains are one type of mountain. They are made when giant blocks of rock are pushed up or pulled apart.

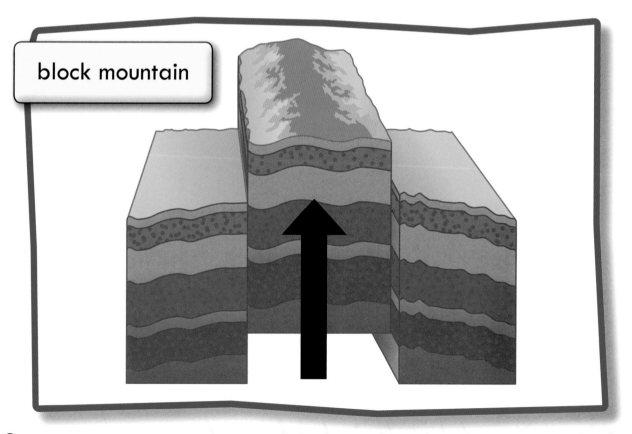

block mountain

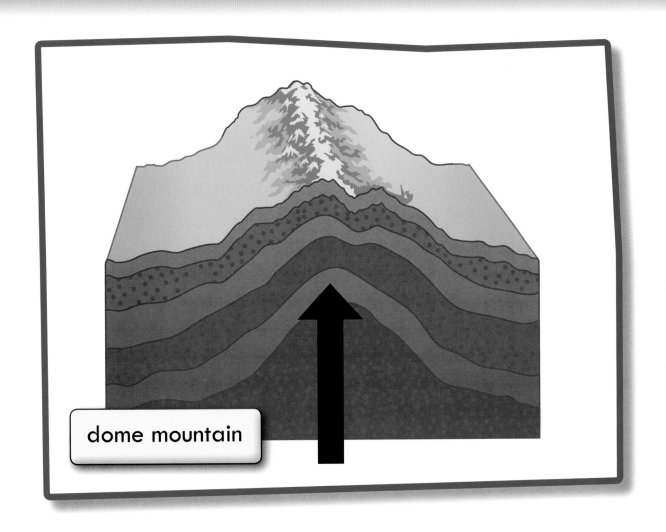

dome mountain

Dome mountains are another type of mountain.
They are made when layers of rock are pushed up
into a dome shape.

Fold mountains

Fold mountains are the most common type of mountain. They are made when layers of rock are scrunched up. Think about how a rug folds if you push it at both ends. That is exactly how fold mountains form, but on a much bigger scale!

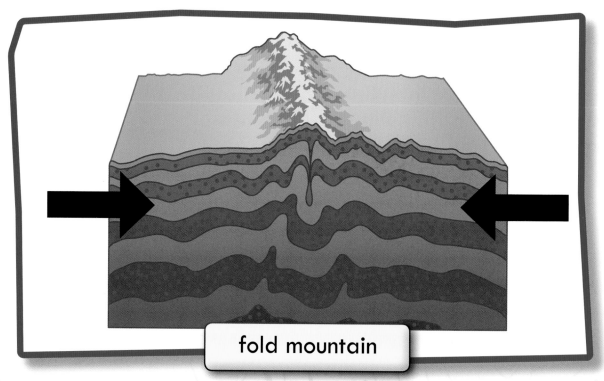

fold mountain

folded rock

Many of the world's major **mountain ranges** are made up of fold mountains. The Andes in South America and the Alps in Europe are fold mountains.

Volcanic mountains

Hot liquid rock called **magma** lies under Earth's **crust.** Sometimes magma forces its way up through the crust and out onto Earth's surface. The magma cools to make new rock that builds up into **volcanoes.**

volcano

The Azores are volcanic islands in the Atlantic Ocean.

Many volcanoes are made under the sea. These are called **seamounts**. When a volcano grows big enough, it rises above the water. Then it becomes a volcanic island.

Wearing mountains away

All mountains are being worn away by **weathering** and **erosion**. Weathering is the breaking up of rocks by the weather.

These jagged mountains have been worn away by weathering and erosion.

loose rock

Erosion happens when loose rock is carried
away. Wind and flowing water blow and wash
away pieces of rocks from mountains into the
valleys below.

Glaciers

Glaciers are huge lumps of ice. As a glacier flows down a mountain slope, it carries chunks of rock with it. These chunks wear away the rocks that the glacier flows over. The glacier carries the broken pieces away.

glacier

This is a U-shaped valley.

As glaciers wear away mountains, they make landforms in the mountains. Over many thousands of years, glaciers create U-shaped valleys, with flat bottoms and steep sides.

Rocks and mountains

There are three types of rocks – igneous, sedimentary and metamorphic. Mountains are made of different rocks.

Sedimentary rock is made up of layers of different rocks.

eroded mountain

Rocks are always changing from one type to another. These changes often happen when mountains are made and worn away.

Mountain climate

On the tops of mountains, the climate is normally cold, wet and windy, even in summer. This pattern of weather is called a mountain climate.

The climate is colder, wetter and windier up the mountain.

valley

The climate on a mountain is different to the climate in the valleys below. The climate is warmer and drier in the valleys below.

Plants and animals

Different plants grow on mountains. As you climb a mountain, you might see grassy meadows, then conifer trees, then alpine plants, then just bare rock and ice, where no plants can survive.

The arctic violet is a tough plant that can survive in mountains.

Mountain goats' hooves are bendy, like rubber, so they can jump from rock to rock.

Animals that can survive in cold, windy conditions live on mountains. For example, mountain goats live in the Rocky Mountains. They have thick woolly coats to keep them warm.

Humans in the mountains

Millions of people live in mountains, even though the weather can be very cold. Many mountain people are farmers. They keep animals such as goats, llamas and yaks.

Farmers grow rice on mountain slopes.

This man lives in the Andes Mountains in Peru, South America.

Mountain life is often tough. There is a lot of snow in winter. This makes it hard for mountain people to travel. There is also a danger of **avalanches**.

Mountains today

Mountains are useful. We get gold and copper from some mountains. Steep-sided valleys are good places to build dams for hydroelectric power stations. A power station makes electricity.

Hydroelectric power station

This man is repairing a mountain footpath in the Lake District

Millions of people also travel to the mountains for skiing, snowboarding, walking, mountain climbing and sightseeing. Unfortunately, some of these activities are causing **erosion**.

Glossary

avalanche slide of snow down a mountain

crust solid, rocky skin of Earth that makes up the surface we stand on

erosion process that wears away rocks and breaks down mountains

glacier slow-moving river of ice that flows down from a mountain

magma hot, melted rock under Earth's crust

mountain range collection of mountains in the same area of the world, such as the Himalayas or the Alps

seamount mountain that rises from the seabed

tectonic plate one of the giant pieces that form Earth's crust

volcano place where magma from beneath Earth's crust comes out onto the surface, often building up a mountain

weathering breaking up of rocks by the weather

Find out more

Books to read

Discover Science: Mountains, Margaret Hynes
(Kingfisher, 2012)

Geography Now: Mountains Around the World,
Jen Green (Wayland, 2012)

Landform Adventures: Cliff Climbers, Anita Ganeri
(Raintree Publishers, 2011)

Websites to visit

**www.bbc.co.uk/science/earth/surface_and_interior/
mountain_formation**
Check out this fantastic video of the Alps Mountains.

**kids.nationalgeographic.co.uk/kids/games/
geographygames/quizyournoodle-mount-everest**
Try this quiz on Mount Everest.

winearth.terc.edu/animations.html
Watch an animation that shows how the Himalayas
were formed.

Index